T0146513

By: William Madison Jr

Stop Don't Buy This Book.............................

Unless You Are Ready for Change

By:

WILLIAM MADISON JR

authorHOUSE®

AuthorHouse™
1663 Liberty Drive
Bloomington, IN 47403
www.authorhouse.com
Phone: 1 (800) 839-8640

Published by AuthorHouse 05/13/2016

ISBN: 978-1-5246-0936-8 (sc)
ISBN: 978-1-5246-0934-4 (hc)
ISBN: 978-1-5246-0935-1 (e)

Library of Congress Control Number: 2016908066

Print information available on the last page.

Contents

Turn up your praise

Acknowledgement

I thank God. I thank my wife, my queen, my best friend, my partner the one and only Tenesha Madison. I thank you baby and I'm so glad I'm married to you. I thank my 4 kids Nia'Mya, Anthony, Christopher and Cameron. I thank my mom and dad. Bertha Madison and William Madison Sr for raising me, for loving me through everything and for always being there for me. I thank my sisters and my nieces & nephew. I thank all my family. I thank all my friends. I thank and appreciate my church family, Sweet Holy Spirit. And I thank any and everyone that has played a part in me becoming the man that I am today. I love you all and I appreciate you. I also want to send a huge shout out and thank you to you, for buying this book and supporting me. I pray that this book adds so much value to you that it blows your mind.

Introduction

My goal in this book is to sell you on you. I have sold crack cocaine, weed, cigarettes, candy, icy cups, basketball cards, cell phone cases, porno movies, clothes, hats, belts, sunglasses, shoes, jewelry, cars and a variety of other things. But now I'm on a mission to sell you on how amazing you really are. My goal is to build your confidence in yourself and in your ability to do, be and have more. My goal is to equip you with a new attitude, a new mindset, that will push you and motivate you to have the lifestyle of your dreams. And I know its possible for you. I have 100% confidence that if you pay attention and apply the principles and values discussed in this book that your life will drastically change and never be the same.

1st Chapter

You Have Options

One of the worst things in the world is to have been brainwashed with the mindset that you do not have any options. Lots of times your environment and the people in which you spend your time with on a regular, will actually have you thinking and feeling as if you have no options. They will throw your limitations at you. They will continually bring up the mistakes you have made in the past, they will bring up your current mistakes you are making & they will predict your future mistakes that you will make. But you need to know that the majority of people actually do not have your best interest at heart, it's a sad reality. You also must understand that your environment can trick you into thinking that your current situation and life style is all you deserve. But I come to tell you with 100% boldness that you in fact do have options. You do not have to play the victim to your environment & circumstances. You do not have to be limited or restricted by the negative feedback and comments of others. Instead you must build

100% confidence in yourself, so that you know that without a shadow of a doubt, you have options. You do not need to be stuck where you are at, when increase, advancement and promotion is available to you. The key principle is you must elevate your mindset and attitude and position your self to receive better circumstances. You must be willing to do more. You must be willing to learn more. You must be willing to be so focused on achieving your goals & dreams that you do not allow anything or anyone to get you distracted. You have been told no, so many times by outside forces that it has caused you to believe that you have no options. Let me explain to you why you have received so many no's. Majority of people are quick to say no because they have been told no, so many times in life. And most people use no as a defense mechanism. The majority of people will say no, not even knowing what they are saying no to, because they have been conditioned and programmed to say no on a regular basis without even having all the information presented to them. No is a form of rejection but you must understand when you receive a no they are not rejecting you personally. They have just been conditioned to repeat what in fact they have received themselves on multiple occasions. So now that you understand the mentality and mindset behind it, please do not allow that to discourage you from achieving everything that is possible for you. I want you to know that you do have options and that you have what it takes to achieve every dream, every goal and every desire.

Another thing you must understand is that you must be passionate, enthusiastic and excited about what you got going on and what you are trying to achieve. You have to know what you want and you must know why you want it. This is so important if you are serious about achieving anything great. People will support you and your vision if you know what you want and why you want it, and if you can communicate it effectively. Because in order to grow and to go to the next level, you are going to have to be willing to put 100% energy and efforts into everything you say and do. You must be so clear and determined as to what you are trying to achieve and why your trying to achieve it. Best advice I can give you on this subject, is to take the time to actually fall in love with your vision, that way when you are sharing your vision (product, service or information.) Whoever you are sharing your vision to, will actually feel the love. And will have an emotional connection because of the love and passion you have shown. Also when you are sharing information or ideas with others, please make sure you look them in the eyes. Make sure your bold, confident and truthful. If someone asks you a question and you do not have an answer, you must have integrity and not lie. Simply be honest and truthful and let them know you will get the correct information or answer to them as soon as possible.

Now on the flip side you can also think you have no other options if you are in fact great at something. Then people and society will play on that and try to limit you to what you are currently doing even if its something you know you do not love 100% and that you know is wrong. Example when I sold drugs everyone told me how much of a hustler I was. They congratulated my successes selling drugs even though I was doing something illegal. Even though I was hurting people and didn't care about people. Just loved making the money and didn't care how I made it or who was hurt in the process. My friends and my environment accepted me and actually had me deceived to the point that I actually thought that there was nothing wrong with what I was doing. There is the notion in the hood that if they don't get the drugs from you, then they will get it from some where else. Then it goes deeper because people will convince you that it's better the addicts get it from you because then at least it's not mixed with anything that's deadly that could really cause harm to the addicts. But that's a trick to have you convinced that what your doing is right when in fact it's 100% wrong. Because drugs are destroying our people. People have lost homes, cars, family, relationships & there minds due to being addicted to drugs. So lets be clear if your selling drugs you are in fact part of the problem.

It takes an enormous amount of energy, skills and work ethic to be successful at selling drugs. My goal for you is that if you are currently reading this and you are a drug dealer. I want you to know that I love you like for real, I love you and I understand where your at but you have to understand if you are a true hustler like you claim to be, then you have the power to switch it up and be way more successful then you are now. All the skills you possess you must put them into something legal and something positive. I'm here to tell you, that you are not a drug dealer. You are in fact an entrepreneur, you are a soon to be successful businessman/woman. You must discover who you are and what you want.

Everyone knows the risk of selling drugs or doing any illegal activities is jail or dead. But we are willing to take that risk because we are risk takers. We are entrepreneurs so the consequences are not enough to really make one want to stop partaking in the illegal activities. The key or principle I should say is for you to ask yourself the tough questions. You know that you are tired of being part of the problem. And inside of you, you want so bad to be part of the solution. You want to make a change. You just don't know how. You feel as if there is so many factors against you. I have been there, I have felt the pain you are feeling. But I have found out and discovered that I in fact have options. And you do to. I have found that people will in fact support my vision, my dream and my goal. And just like you are reading my book right now. This was one of my goals and the fact that you are reading it now is proof that change is possible. The fact that you are still reading and thinking that you are ready for a change is proof that you will receive the love and support you need to make the changes in your life so that you can be successful financially, physically, spiritually, emotionally, and mentally. This is just the beginning for you and I'm excited. Let's win because we got what it takes.

I'm sitting here thinking about when I was selling cars out of 30 different salesmen, each month I was either #1, #2, #3 or #4. The car business was a very competitive and hectic line of work. We were taught and trained to not get the customers the best deals because the better deal the customer got the less money we will make in commissions as a salesman. We were taught to upsale warranties. We were taught to charge extra for different features. We were taught on the financing part to get extra points as far as higher interest rate then banks quoted. (Usually banks will pay higher to dealerships if finance manager can get customer to agree at a point or 2 or 3 points higher interest rate.)

So a little advice if you are buying a used car in the future and your quoted for example 12% interest rate, chances are you can negotiate that down 1-3% so always keep that in mind. Usually everything is negotiable not just in the car business but in life in general. So keep that in mind and always try to get the best deal and best value.

It's amazing when I was selling cars everyone told me how great of a car salesman I was. They congratulated me and I even had sales managers tell me that I was born to sell cars. (Notice the environment and people will try to make you think you have no options. Can be on the negative or positive. Because majority of people will try to control your destiny, if you let them.) I was a victim to this cycle for years because they had me trained to think that this was my only option because I had been a drug dealer and I had multiple felonies and I had did 4½ years in the penitentiary. (I will tell you my experiences there in another chapter. Let's stay focused on this you have options. LOL)

I know as your reading this you are thinking about certain people or your environment and you can start to see how they might be trying to hinder your growth or hinder the changes that you want to make but are a little scared to make. (I know you thinking you are not scared of anything, yeah that's what your mouth says but your actions are saying something different. It's all love.)

You have to not get upset at them because surprisingly enough some people put limits and labels on you. And they think they are doing you a favor. They think they are showing love. And majority of them actually believe that they have no options also, so that type of mentality and mindset can be contagious. But you are going to break the cycle because you are discovering that you in fact do have options. This is the beginning process, this is the birthplace for change. This is the exciting part, realizing that more is available.

Sitting here thinking there are so many beautiful women with nice bodies and attitudes. And they use there bodies to get them favor, indirectly most times. Some times intentional, but never the less using the body as a tool to get what they want, when they want it. Ladies you are amazing. You are beautiful, and the love that you possess on the inside is like no other. Ladies I want you to know that no matter what's going on in your life, that you should be respected and appreciated for all that you do. So I salute you all. I want you to know that you in fact do have options. Do not allow a man to belittle you or put limits on you. You can be secure with yourself and with your abilities. Remember you are designed to be great, not because you have something to prove. But because you are great inside and out. Ladies you are special in every way. Do yourself a favor and never underestimate yourself. You do not have to doubt yourself because you have special insight that allows you to make the necessary connections to bring about change in your life. I want you to know I love you and I honor you. Ladies you birth our children. Ladies you are loving and caring. Sometimes your attitude can get you in trouble. LOL Ladies I have some advice for you. If you are in a relationship it's extremely important that you encourage and motivate your man. It's important that yall be committed to working as a team. Because yall our partners and the goal is for yall to achieve both of yall goals, dreams and desires. Ladies I want yall to win, I want yall to be the best women, the best mothers, the best sisters and the best examples of what it means to be a phenomenal women. You hold the power to make things right. So be loving, be nice and be supportive at all times.

Its so important that as were discovering and realizing that we do have options, that we be encouraged and motivated through the change process. Because any time there is a change, there is also the possibility of going back to the familiar situation. Because the unknown present's a false fear that will make you think that with a change there is no guarantee that things will work out. But you must realize that if you remain focused and do not allow yourself to get distracted. Then you are positioning yourself and your family and everyone connected to you to be in a much better situation that you could actually be proud about. Remember broken things can be fixed. Remember pain is only temporary. Remember when you know for yourself that you in fact do have options, that will give you the confidence to attack everyday and every assignment with enthusiasm, determination and a winning mindset. You have the power to change your situation. You have the power to go after what you really want to do. If you have not figured it out yet. Then take some time now and start thinking about it. Jot you some notes down and ask yourself some tough questions you been meaning to ask yourself but it seems like you never have any time because you are to busy doing things that you assumed was priority, that you assumed was important, which in the past it actually was. But now your searching for your purpose because you want to be fulfilled. So take some time to think, answer some of your own questions and then formulate a game plan. Now is your time to shine. Now is your season, I'm so excited for you. Keep reading and as you are reading keep thinking. You are about to go to the next level. Promotion and increase is yours.

If you are working at a job and it's been stagnate and your pay or responsibilities have not increased. Now is the time to be willing to do more than what your currently paid for because that's the only way you will get recognized. If you are working for someone ask the owner, in what way can you be more valuable. You must have a strong work ethic to get ahead. Rather you own a company or work for a company. You must have integrity about yourself. Make it a habit of doing what you say you are going to do. If you work for someone they should not have to tell you 2 or 3 times to do a particular task. You have to be on top of your business in every way if you really truly want to get ahead. Another point is you have to know when your time is up at a place as well. Because after you have exhausted all your efforts and you are doing everything in your power to do your best but your still getting treated unfairly. Then you have to be willing to analyze yourself and your situation so you can discover what's the best options for you and your family. Because you are not stuck, you do have options.

I can relate to business owners because I had a successful lawncare/ landscaping company for 8 years. And if you are working for a company just like you have options to quit that company and go some where else. The owner also got options because there are so many people looking for work. So you can be replaced easily. The truth of the matter is a lot of times doing just your job and doing the minimum and what's just required of you will not cut it. If you work for a company you must be willing to put 100% energy and effort into your daily assignments. If you are a worker for a company you must have the mindset and attitude to want to see the company grow. Because if you are a key reason for the growth then you best believe your going to get promoted and more money is coming your way. Plus you are preparing yourself to own your own business one day. I personally believe it should be everyone's goal to be a business owner because the most financially successful people in the world own businesses and or real estate and or investments. So even if you are working for a company and you love it, you should still consider having a business on the side as well. You have so many options to how you can make it work. Do not ever limit yourself because you have the ability to achieve anything that you are willing to work for. When I had my lawncare service I experience so many people that worked for me just to get a check. You can not have this mind set, if you are working for a company you must do something you enjoy. You should wake up every morning excited to go to work because you love what you do. If you do

11

not love what you are currently doing then you must take some time to analyze your self and your situation. The goal is to wake up everyday excited about your day because your working on your goals, dreams and the vision you have for your life. Its possible to absolutely love what you do 100%. It's possible to be 100% happy with your work, yourself and your current situation. Remember joy, peace, wealth, and happiness is available to you. The whole reason for wanting increase in every area of your life is to give you more options. Because when you realize that you actually have options, something magical takes place in the inside of you that will infact boost your confidence and position you to have the life style of your dreams. Remember success in every single area of your life is available to you. As you are reading this, things are starting to click for you. Do me a favor and do not beat yourself up for any mistakes you have made in the past. They were necessary and they were all part of your journey. But you have a responsibility to change certain things about yourself, when you have encountered new information that will infact add value to your life. New information is what changes lives. 1 book can make the world of difference. And I believe if you apply the principles, values, mindset and attitude discussed in this book that your life will change and never be the same.

2nd Chapter

Mindset and Attitude That Will Lead to Change

Most people don't see anything wrong with there mindset or attitude thus here is no need for change. But the fact remains if you are not consistently winning then you need to make some adjustments. If you are not getting the desired results in every area of your life then you need to make some adjustments. If you are not excited every single day when you wake up, then your mindset and attitude needs some adjustments. Most people think it's not possible to wake up everyday excited about life, excited about what you are working on. I come to tell you that it is in fact possible. You must discover how and why that's the challenge. The majority of people live with themselves but don't truly know themselves. Because they have not took time to sit down and analyze self. Majority of people want everyone else to change but you must take some time to analyze yourself and figure out, what it is you need to change about yourself. This is so so very important.

Everyone wants an opportunity, but I tell people all the time, if you are not prepared for that opportunity, then the very opportunity you been waiting on, will in fact make a fool of you, if you are not properly prepared. Everyone wants to be successful, I hear it all the time. But alot of people have to understand, what's your reasoning behind wanting to be so successful. What's your why? That's what you must realize first, what is the reason as to why you want to be successful. Because if you do not know your why then 9 times out of 10 its not going to happen. You can not go about your day aimlessly. You must write down what you want to achieve. And then be willing to put forth 100% energy and efforts into making it happen. You must have a mindset to shut down any and all distractions that are trying to hinder your growth. The number 1 reason majority of people lack confidence is because they continue to loose. When you experience lost after lost after lost after lost that can take a major blow on your confidence and your self-esteem. Thus making you feel inadequate and unworthy. But the beautiful thing is new information can allow you to shift your mindset and attitude.

Women have it so hard because society portrays so many images of what the perfect woman is suppose to look like and act like. So woman can find themselves comparing themselves to celebrities and not even be fully aware of it. Another point I must mention ladies and fellas you must love yourself. Everyone assumes that they love themselves. The true test to see if you truly love yourself is, do you truly 100% enjoy and appreciate your own company. Or do you feel the need to always be around someone else. You must take time to love on your self. Take yourself to the movies, take your self to a nice restaurant, take yourself to get your nails, and feet done. Spend time with yourself getting to know yourself. You should be 100% comfortable when you are alone. This is an important principle, I hope you are paying attention. We have to decide to love ourselves everyday. It's a decision we must make each and everyday if we are going to have the right mindset and attitude that leads to success in each and every area of our lives.

Another principle that has truly shifted my mindset and attitude is the get to/got to. This is a concept that will shift your perspective. Instead of saying for example I got to get the kids ready, I got to go to work, I got to go to school, I got to pay all these bills or whatever the case may be. When we say we got to do something, in the inside of us it's presented as a burden. But when we say we get to for example get the kids ready, we get to go to work, we get to go to school, we get to pay bills or whatever the case may be. When we say we get to then it's presented as an opportunity. This concept has literally changed my life. It makes me feel so much better when I say I get too. And I'm sure it will have the same affect on you. So from know on you get to, ok.

Another principle is majority of people say "I can't afford that." When you say you cant afford something, that shuts down any possibility for you to figure out a way to afford it. But when you say "How can I afford it," that opens up so many different possibilities in the mind that will allow you to be creative to figure out a way to afford the very thing you are trying to afford.

In order to have a change in mindset and attitude, I suggest you try to encourage everyone you come in contact with. I challenge you, because if you commit to doing this your life will change and never be the same. We as people must genuinely love each other, support each other and encourage each other.

You can not let the pressures of life, way you down. The key is to be solution oriented and not problem oriented. You have the power to change your situation and your life. It starts with the decision to live life on your own terms. It starts with making a declaration that you have messed up time and time before and you are now ready and receptive to new mindset and new attitude towards yourself and towards everyone else.

One thing that has truly helped me, is I respect everyone's differences and I always have the mindset that we all need each other. So if you can shift your mindset to not judge one another because of financial status or education status. It will level the playing field and will allow you to treat everyone with love and respect because we are all important. We just do things differently. My desire is for you to be successful in each and every area of your life. I am personally so glad that I was able to shift my mindset and attitude from that of a successful drug dealer, to that of a successful businessman/entrepreneur. I'm so glad that I'm in a position now to help people and not hurt people. I'm so glad that now I'm in fact part of the solution and not part of the problem. I now have a few successful businesses, none of which requires me to hurt people and sell posion to profit.

Another thing is you must congratulate yourself for small wins because this will boost your confidence. And in order for us to be effective in everything we do and say, we must be confident. You must beware of excitement killers. These are people who will try to kill your excitement, when you are excited about an idea or what you got going on. Remember majority of people think what they have going on is more important than what you are working on. So keep that in mind when you conversate with people. In order for us to be effective, we must learn and listen to people. This learned skill will set you up for much success.

I'm at a point now where I literally wake up with the mindset to make a difference in everyone's life, I come in contact with. Life is so much more fulfilling when you have discovered your purpose in life and when you have a vision and assignment to fulfill and you are working towards your goals and dreams everyday.

I can tell you now if you have figured out your purpose in life then you are part of the 10% that have discovered it, because 90% of people have not found it out. Also if you have not discovered your purpose yet, then you need to take some time to try to figure it out. What makes you smile? What makes you cry? What pisses you off when someone is doing it wrong, that you know how to do right? What would you do for free? What do you absolutely love doing? Ask yourself these questions and more and soon you will discover what your purpose is. You must take the time to figure out, who you are, what you want and then formulate a game plan on how to get it. You must understand you are amazing and there is no one else in the world exactly like you. Actually take a moment, smile right now. Look in the mirror and tell yourself that you love yourself and give yourself any other compliments you would like too, its ok.

I have been doing this for years. At first it seems a little strange and weird but the more you do it, the more powerful it is. We must constantly sell ourselves, on ourselves. (Will talk more about this in a few chapters) We must utilize our time most effectively. We can not just talk about how successful we want to be, we must be willing to put the work in to be successful in every area of our live. Everyone talks a good game, few execute. We must be about that action and not all talk. Majority of people have a plan and know what they want to do, but still are not doing it. So that's proof knowing is not enough. You must execute in order to be effective in your chosen field. Do not let fear stop you from going after something that you really want to achieve.

Quick story, I had a fear of heights so what I did was, I wanted to face that fear. So guess what I did? Yes I jumped out of a perfectly good airplane from 14,000 feet. Wish I could tell you everything went perfect and I conquered it with ease. Nope it didn't go down that way. I watched the video's, I was prepared mentally. I got harnessed in and I actually surprisingly was not that nervous. I got in the plain and as the plane got higher and higher, I talked to myself repeatedly and I was fully prepared. Soon as I get to 14,000 feet, the instructor instructed me it was time to jump. I looked down, smiled and jumped out of a perfectly good airplane from 14,000 feet. But I forgot to breathe and actually panicked. I thought I was going to die, I couldn't breathe, my head was hurting and the gear was on to tight. I was totally uncomfortable, I felt sick and did not enjoy the process. But guess what I still did it and the moral of the story is I overcame the fear. And now anytime fear tries to creep up, I shut the fearful thought down, by using the example to myself that I was able to jump out of a plane from 14,000 feet and I survived it.

It's so important to pull on our previous experiences as motivation to conquer what we come against, that's why we must apply all that we have learned through the years. (Will discuss this in great detail in a few chapters.)

The key to being successful and having the right winning attitude and mindset. Is you must have a set of principles and values that you live by each and everyday. You must set a standard of excellence for yourself and you must be disciplined enough to stick to that standard. Actually make a declaration to yourself right now, that you will no longer loose, but instead you will win or learn. Having that type of mindset will take away the fear of starting new tasks that appear to be hard.

When I think about fear, I think about expecting something bad to happen that 9 times out of 10 will not even happen. So continue to build confidence in yourself and your abilities and the fears will disappear. Another principle is you must have an attitude of gratitude at all times. You must live in such a way that you and everyone you come in contact with knows without a shadow of a doubt that you are so grateful and appreciative to be alive and well and in the land of the living.

Do me a favor. Make a commitment to yourself that for the next 30 days, you will be 100% committed to being nice to any and everyone you come in contact with. This is a call to action.

Another thing is if you are serious about change. You are going to have to stop being so mean. If you shut down that mean attitude and replace it with a nice loving attitude. Then I assure you being extra nice will take care of you and position you to get all of your heart's desires.

If you will be 100% faithful its so many benefits that comes along with that. You can not take advantage of people because it will come back to bite you. Ladies love and respect your man and really treat him like a king. Fellas love and respect your woman and really treat her like a queen. If you pick right then it should be no reason for you to cheat on your partner. Instead work together, enjoy each other and appreciate each other. You do not have to compare other couples relationship with yours. Instead use your energy to help each other. Be good to each other. Relationships can be extremely challenging because you got 2 totally different people coming together. With different personalities, attitudes, upbringings, ways of thinking, lifestyles and mindsets. The key is to be willing to work together and to be 100% faithful to each other. It's to complicated to fool around with multiple partners, and it's not right.

Let me share a little bit about myself. I have lied, cheated, stole, misused people, broke the law on several occasions, sold drugs and did a variety of other things that were wrong. We all know right from wrong in most cases but somehow, we all have collectively choose wrong on several occasions. We know that doing wrong has consequences but yet in still we still do wrong. We have too much at stake, that's why being open to change is so important. I'm so glad that I have made the changes in my life. Now I'm seeing the benefits from living right.

I used to be a big gambler. I wasted thousands of dollars on lottery and at casino boats. I'm so glad that I don't have them bad habits anymore. My desire to wanting to be part of the solution is stronger than the desire to wanting to be part of the problem. Now it's easy to shut down wrong habits because I have built a level of discipline, that allows me to live by a set of values and principles.

It's crazy because I actually did 4½ years in the penitentiary due to selling crack cocaine, weed and cigarettes. I also have been robbed or attempted to be robbed about 6 times in the past. I have been selfish and cared more about money than people in the past. I have lusted after women with big booties, nice titties and pretty faces. I have mismanaged money for years. I have caused hurt to people that love me. I'm jaked up and messed up in more ways than one. But I'm so grateful, so very thankful for the changes I have made. Its truly a major difference, and I'm so proud of myself.

If you are reading this, I want you to know that change is possible for you. You owe it to yourself to make the necessary changes so that you can actually start living your best life now. By me doing 4½ yrs in the penitentiary I picked up a bad habit of masturbating everyday and lusting after woman. An addiction that took me years to get under control. The flesh has desires that seem to be uncontrollable, when that addiction is in you. But I'm here to tell you that it's possible to stop lusting and masturbating after women. It's wrong and you know its wrong, so if you are currently doing it and caught in that cycle. You must discipline yourself to shut down the fleshly desires, so you can gain control over yourself and over your life. This addiction is causing you more harm than it has good. Fellas I suggest finding the right woman that compliments you well and then marrying her so that yall can satisfy each others needs. Ladies I suggest finding the right man that respects you, loves you, teaches you, provides and appreciates you and then marrying him so that yall can satisfy each others needs. If we are to grow and develop and be successful in every area of our lives, then we are going to have to have a burning desire to want to live right and be right. We can not continue to do wrong and expect right to come from wrong. Instead make the decision to change your mindset and attitude and do what's right, live by principles and values that govern your life and watch your life change and never be the same. I'm excited for you, I love you and want the absolute best for you. Remember the goal is to be whole and successful mentally, physically, spiritually, financially and emotionally.

3rd Chapter

Knowing the Author/My Story

My name is William D. Madison Jr, I am currently 32 years old. Married with 4 kids. My wife Tenesha Madison is the best wife in the world. I am so grateful to have such a phenomenal woman to call my wife. My kids are 13, 6, 3 and new born. (Nia'Mya, Anthony, Christopher, Cameron) You know they keep me busy. I am a family man. I love God and I love people. I wake up everyday with the attitude and mindset to encourage, inspire and empower people. I am making a difference in the lives of people and it feels so good to be a part of the solution and not the problem. It feels so good to be in a position to help people and not hurt people. I'm just so humbled and grateful that I'm able to do what I do every day. I literally have encounters everyday where I'm able to help people and I do not take it for granted. I wake up everyday excited, because I'm blessed to love what I do. My desire is to be a blessing to everyone I come in contact with. I go on the streets everyday to motivate people. Because we all hurt in one way or another, so a word of encouragement and motivation can make all the difference. It's so important that I am 100% committed to the cause and to the work I do everyday. Turn Up Your Praise Ministry is an outreach ministry. Where we are making a difference, in different communities. I feed and clothe the homeless twice a month, and I love it. Ministry has its challenges because you see so many people hurting and bound by addictions and vices. You want to just help everyone because people are going through some really hard times. Some people are loosing faith, loosing hope, some people are loosing jobs, cars, homes, husbands, wives, businesses, loosing self respect and a variety of other things because its so much going on. My heart ways heavy lots of days because I wish I could do more, but I'm joyed because I am doing my part. And I'm making a difference, so I do know God is pleased with me. I just want to live right and be a blessing. I have a burning desire to please God. I grew up with my mom, dad, and 2 sisters. I was the only boy. I had a pretty good childhood my mom and dad took really good care of us. I honor and respect them for being great. They argue and fuss but they love each other and they are still married. I respect that so much, through all they been through, they still married. You know we live in an age where majority of marriages don't even last 5 years, so the fact that my parents are still together is a blessing. My father taught me the importance of work ethic and hustling and for that I will be for ever thankful. My dad was a cab driver at ED's livery on 94th and state in

Chicago IL. Before CTA bought it. My father left out every morning at 6:30 AM and didn't return until 7:30 PM. My father provided and I saw him work hard everyday of my life. My mother took care of all the house duties and did everything for us to make sure we were straight. At an early age of 8 years old I started selling icy cups, candy and basketball cards. I understood the importance of earning money and I made money everyday. I even cut grass, shoveled snow, pulled weeds and did a variety of other things to earn money. I kept a pocket full of money and I been hustling my entire life. As I sit here writing I'm thinking about all the stuff I have sold through the years to earn money.

As a young boy with my candy store and coming to school with a gym bag full of candy every single day. (In which I sold out everyday.) I sold so many different things and it eventually lead me to selling weed in the 8th grade. I would hide $5 nickel bags of weed inside of 2 deodorant sticks. I had a great connect and I was making money. Eventually picked up a gambling habit where I shot dice every day and sold weed. At the time I enjoyed the life style, I enjoyed the money, I enjoyed the power, the status and the influence I had. I eventually progressed to selling crack cocaine. I was making alot of money and selling wholesale also. I was fronting drugs to anyone who had a little hustle in them. I ended up graduating high school June 2002. Then I started drug trafficking back and forward from Chicago to Wisconsin. I had got to the point where I was buying a key of cocaine and breaking it down and selling it in bags and in ounces in Lacrosse Wisconsin. I had business set up in Chicago running smoothly and I had it set up in Lacrosse, Wisconsin running smoothly. I was supposedly living the life, making good illegal money that people dreamed of making. I had been making 10,000 a week. I had money coming in so fast I hid money in banks, safe deposit boxes, ceilings, dresser draws, under carpets, ceilings, garages. I remember putting money everywhere. Had so many different stashes. One evening I was in Lacrosse and got pulled over they didn't catch any drugs on me but I had 15,000 cash on me. And I had a piece of paper in my pocket with some names of people who owed me thousands and had some gun information. I was able to come into the small town and take over rather fast. I supplied everyone with crack cocaine. I was moving fast and making mistakes. I had thousands and thousands of drugs fronted out. And was selling like crazy. Eventually I got caught up because a addict wore a wire on me and got me set up. They caught me with 10 ounces of crack cocaine and thousands of dollars. I was now 18 yrs old and its Oct 2002 and I finally got caught up. I thought I would never get caught. When I was in Lacrosse County Jail when news came on they had me featured as a small city drug Lord. My bond was 25,000 cash. So I got on the pay phone telling my parents where to go get the cash from my stashes. They came the next day and bonded me out and then I was back down. Had to go to court in 2 weeks. I leave from Chicago headed back to Lacrosse Wisconsin to go to court. I'm in the elevator, I holds the door open for the police officer and he cuffs me up and throws me in County Jail. Comes to find out they recorded phone calls and had me on tape saying where to get the money from my stashes. I got a lawyer from Chicago paid him 7,500 cash and he gets down to court in Lacrosse and he is stuttering and everything and talking about best they can offer is 5 yrs in and 10 years on paper. I wasn't going for that so I got a lawyer from down in Lacrosse Wisconsin, it was a lawyer that the judge knew. So I thought I was going to get off on this case. Paid the new lawyer 3,500 cash. The County Jail was horrible they had us sleeping on solid concrete. Was fights in the day room all the time. The food sucked and I was not feeling that place at all. I was ready go, I was ready to get out of there. So crazy enough the lawyer worked out for me that I could get boot camp. I was like bet, I was in the County Jail fighting the case for almost a year so boot camp was cool. I was with it anything to get out of the county, because the guys in the block had already said on multiple occasion as how much better the joint was. So I was ready to go to the joint or boot camp or anything. By the time I got sentenced I was suppose to get boot camp but instead ended up getting 2½ yrs in and 3½ yrs out and was able to transfer everything back to Chicago upon my release. So I knocked out the time like a champ. I read, I worked out everyday and I played spades, and domino's. The penitentiary experience was not that bad at all. It sucked to be in that controlled environment but it was honestly not as bad as I expected. So I did all my time knocked it out like a champ. Getting released was like the best feeling in the world. Sweet freedom, I was too geeked. Now I was on papers and adjusting to being back home. I was out for 60 days, I had a gambling problem. I ended up loosing like almost 2,000 at the boat and I was sick then I got back in the neighborhood. Got word that the connect had some purple fluffy med grade that was like vacuumed sealed, no seeds some pure good bud from California or Arizona. Any way I was backed down through being locked up first through bond money being snatched, lawyer fees & people that owed me from me fronting, I was at a 200,000 lost. So this time I was determined to bounce back smart. I wasn't going to fool around with no crack cocaine. I was just going to mess with the weed. So everything was going great I had gotten to copping 20 pounds at a time. Sales were going great, money was flowing, I was back rolling and living good. I had even made a connection with an Arab and I was getting new port cigarettes at $2 a pack so I was buying 10,000 packs every 2 weeks. Indiana had them for like $3.50 a pack and in Chicago they were $5-$6 a pack. So I was winning I was selling pounds & ounces of weed. And I was wholesaling cartoons of new ports to stores and cigarette houses. Money was flowing super fast. Funny story I meet the Arab guy at dunkin donuts to pick up another 10,000 packs of new ports and like 12 police cars pullin. I said dang I'm busted. But it just so happened we were meeting at the dunkin donuts and cops like donuts, it was just a coincidence. And my cigarette connect brother owned the dunkin donuts so everything was love. I was just paranoid. I thought I was doing everything right this time. Everyone knows if you get caught with weed or cigarettes you not getting no time. So I thought I was scott free this time. I assumed this was the lick for me.

But one things for sure and two things are for certain you can not continue to do wrong and expect good to come out of it. So adventually I got my parents house raided and they caught me with 22½ pounds of weed and like 9,830 packs of new port. This time I got sentenced to 2 years in and 3 years out. (Total of 4½ yrs in penitentiary and 3 years on parole I did.) This time when I got looked up I did some soul searching and made the necessary changes to live right. While incarcerated I was granted an opportunity to go to a work release center for my last year. So after I got to work release center and got situated and everything, I was granted access to go look for a job. I ended up getting hired at a car dealership on Western Avenue and I worked there everyday from 9 AM to 8 PM so my time flew pass. I was able to stack some legal money. I was committed to turning over a new leaf. So I kept the job even after my release. I still worked at dealership for several years. I thank God for that dealership because I meet my lovely wife there. And it taught me the importance of having great credit and all the benefits. I truly learned alot from that place. Out of 30 salesman, every month I got 1st place, 2nd place, 3rd place or 4th place. I proved myself to be one of the best there surely. But I still was being treated unfairly and it was to much shady stuff going on.

I was able to buy a house for me and my family in the suburbs and things were going smooth. I was making around 80,000 a year and I was making side bird dogs and referrals from sending customers to other dealerships, so that was like an extra 1,000 a month in bird dogs and referral checks. I was tired of selling cars, it wasn't for me. The final straw was when I sold a lady an "04" GMC Envoy the lady's grandma had signed the car loan. We sold it at $14,000 and interest rate was like 8% so it was a good deal. I made like a $600 commission on it but one day the finance manager called me into office and said we had to resign the lady and when we got through resigning the lady the car went to $18,000 for same car and like 15% interest rate, my commission went up to like $1,400 and dealership made rest of money. The lady car note went up like almost 300 bucks extra per month for 5 or 6 years. It was wrong on so many different levels. From finance & dealership perspective as long as they resigned that's all that mattered. I hated that deal and that was the final straw. So I then quit from what was basically an almost 6 figure a year job. I wanted to be my own boss. I was an entrepreneur, so I stepped out in faith and started a lawncare service.

And for my advertising I wrote a handwritten letter and it worked. I had spoke from the heart and people supported left and right. Lawncare services was growing I had gotten to the point where I had 4 work vans and 3 vans out cutting. It came with many challenges. At that time I was also able to buy my first rental property. It is now rented out and has residual income coming on. As the lawncare services was growing, I had started selling knockoff designer handbags, belts, book bags, shoes, sunglasses etc. So that money started coming so fast and it's easier with product businesses to manage than with service businesses. Plus I was having some challenges with my lawn care staff. So I decide to downsize the lawncare and rapidly grow the knock off business. So that's what I did I was selling purses, wallets, belts, shoes etc to all the hustlers in Chicago land area and surrounding suburbs. Things were going smooth. I was cutting grass everyday and selling the knockoffs for years. I was making 3,000-4,000 per month with lawncare, I was making 4,000-12,000 per month with selling knockoffs and I was making $950 month from rental property. Money was flowing good but I was still not satisfied because I still knew within myself that I was doing wrong. I was rushing through cutting of the yards, doing mediocre jobs, just rushing through the motions. I was committing illegal activities still because I was selling knockoff designer merchandise and even though no one else told me it was wrong. I knew it was wrong. I was tired, I had a strong desire within me to start my own brand. I had a strong desire to encourage people because I saw so many people hurting in one area or another. So I stepped out in faith and literally just ended a successful lawncare service and ended a successful knock off designer business. Now I'm doing what I love every day and even though it has some challenges, I absolutely love it and I'm committed 100% to making a difference in the lives of others. My goal is to help you succeed in every area of your life. My goal is for you to be whole. My goal is for you to have no stress, no drama and no confusion. It's possible, be encouraged and know that you got what it takes to achieve every goal, every dream, every vision and every assignment for your life.

I get so much joy in motivating and encouraging people. I love people and I'm committed to making this world a better place. I am now part of the solution. I am now successful in every area of my life. I want us to continue to win. I want us to love, encourage and support each other. We are all connected and we need each other. I want to thank you again for supporting this book. I pray that it's adding value to you. So be encouraged and continue to read its about to get intense. Now you know about me, I'm glad I was able to share my journey with you. I'm in a great place right now. I'm excited, passionate and enthusiastic about everything that I'm working on. Now enough about me this next chapter is about to blow your mind and I'm 100% sure if you apply the principles and values to your life then your life will change and never be the same. So get ready, get ready, get ready

4th Chapter

Sell Yourself on Yourself Everyday

Everyday we are being bombarded with approximately 2,000 ads. When you turn on tv, phone, radio, internet, social media sites no matter where you are you will have ads and signs trying to sell you something. Down every expressway is Big Billboards soliciting you to buy something. You must be aware of the worlds system. The world is trying its best to sell you. But you must ask yourself. Are you selling yourself on yourself everyday? If you get this concept, then your life will change and never be the same. The answer to your problems is in selling yourself. You have to be fully persuaded and fully convinced on how amazing you are. Even if you're in the process of bettering your self and in the process of learning new things and making adjustments to have a better quality of life. Just like you wake up everyday and brush your teeth. You must wake up everyday and sell yourself. If you are not doing this already, every single day then this is one of the main reason that you are not getting the results you desire. This is a life changing principle and when you make it a daily habit you will start to see a change in every area of your life. Compliment yourself, fall in love with yourself because you are phenomenal and the fact remains there is no one in the world exactly like you. When you are 100% sold on yourself then you won't need the approval of others. When you make selling yourself everyday, a lifestyle you position yourself to see things differently. You position yourself to seize great opportunities. And you also position yourself to not being taken advantage of on a regular basis. Once you truly discover who you are and you discover how amazing and wonderful you are. It will build up confidence within you to the point where you will know with 100% certainty that you got what it takes to be successful in every area of your life. You will also see the world differently and you will respect selling more. Because in order to achieve any great level of success you will have to sell yourself. You will have to communicate your ideas effectively. You must understand your products or services in order to be effective as you are in the selling process. Remember you are always selling rather you realize it or not. The key principle is to make sure you sell yourself on yourself every single day. That will allow you to have the right perspective to be effective on your job or in your business or with your relationships and with anything that you are working on. I'm going to share with you in this chapter some key tips that will help you. But first I have to challenge you to sell yourself on yourself every single day. This is not a 30 day challenge or a 90 day challenge, this is a until you die challenge. Because this principle is so important that you must incorporate it into your daily activities. It must become a part of you. Just as surely as you are connected to your name. You must have the same connection to selling yourself on yourself every single day, this is the best advice I can give you because I know once implemented every day. Your life will change and you will be forever grateful for this principle. It has changed my life and I'm 100% sure it will change yours as well, if you make the decision to do it every single day. If you really want change, if you really want more out of life and more out of yourself then you must accept this challenge and be 100% focused and watch how things start to change rapidly in your life for the better.

For many selling is one of the hardest things to do, even when it's being done directly or indirectly all day everyday. My goal is for you to see selling differently, so you can be aware and conscious of different strategies and techniques, so you can apply them to your job or your business and you will be more effective and get much better results.

After you get into the habit of selling yourself everyday in yourself, it will allow you to be more comfortable as you are selling others. (People love to buy but hate to be sold.) It's so important that you be intentional as you are trying to sell your products or services. You have to be a little aggressive but never be overly aggressive it will turn a customer off so fast. Will discuss some great strategies and techniques in a future chapter. Everyone needs a best friend, I tell people that when you truly fall in love with yourself then you should be your own best friend. That will position you to be a better friend to the people that are a part of your life. Whatever we make priority and important in life is what will manifest in our lives. We live in an age of social media and pictures. So what happens is most people are directly or indirectly comparing themselves to other people on social sites based off of pictures. Yes we all heard the saying a picture is worth 1,000 words, we also must understand that even though a picture does have great value, a picture can also be deceiving. Because we live in an era of filters and editing so in most cases what you actually see has been altered. So in essence you are comparing yourself and your situation to something that has been altered. These are things you must be aware of because your value should not come from the opinions of others. You are phenomenal and amazing regardless if anyone else see's it or not. (Side note; if everyone is complaining about you, then you could actually be the problem lol in which ever case. You can change your situation and the perspective in which others see you. By selling yourself on yourself everyday. Then that confidence will make other people respect you more and appreciate you more, because now you respect and appreciate yourself more because you know your worth.)

You must develop a strong sense of the power you have to change any situation. You also must keep your word. When you say your going to do something, you must do it. Having integrity is so very important in the selling yourself process. The majority of people do not like making commitments because then they feel obligated to do whatever needs to be done. But if you are serious about being successful in every area of your life, you are going to have to make some commitments and you are going to have to stick to them. It's no getting around it, so just start getting comfortable making commitments.

See before I learned this principle, the image I had of myself was based on the worlds perspective of me and not my own. That's why I say this principle is so powerful, so life changing because now I know how powerful I am, now I know my worth, my value and now I can go out boldly and be effective with everything I do and say. That's why thousands of people can tell me no everyday and it will not have an effect on me, because I do not take it personally. And I receive so many yes's and I understand you have to go through no's to get to yes's. So many people quit after receiving multiple no's because they are not 100% sold on their products or services. If you know within yourself that your products or services will make a difference in the lives of others you should never allow a no to stop you. Rather you work for a company or you own the company, you should always be promoting and marketing your products and/or services. People have to know who you are and what you do. I truly believe that people are looking for your products or services. So you must open up your mouth and share with everyone who you are and what you do. This is so important if you are serious about growth and going to the next level. Remember sales and profit is the lifeline of any business so if you are not promoting and selling then you are setting yourself up for failure and in essence you are killing your business. Remember in life and in business you are either growing or dying at all times. You are either progressing or your stagnate. You must make every attempt to get better in your life and in your business. Do not disrespect yourself or your business by slacking and not sharing with everyone, what you got going on. Also remember to achieve success in business and in every area of your life you must be a servant. Because truly successful people serve. The more people you serve, the more your brand will be recognized in your market place. So stay humble at all times and always have the mindset and desire to make your customers feel special and important because if it wasn't for them you wouldn't be in business. So continue to love and appreciate your customers. Also you should be consistently marketing to your current customers that love you, to send you some referrals. (Friends and family that would love your products or services and would love to do business with you.) Also remember being a pushy salesman is never good. You must show the value of your products or services because when perceived value exceeds the cost, then a sale will usually be made. So always share the benefits of your products or services. In a sales process an emotional connection must be made, will discuss more in next chapter.

Another thing you never know who your customer knows. And remember one customer can lead to millions in sells. So act as if each customer can be that one. This tip is so valuable because it will force you to have phenomenal customer service at all times. Which is what it takes to get to the next level

And what it takes to remain successful as well. Again I say, you must believe in yourself 100% and you must believe in your product or service 100% or your customers will pick up on that and it will lead to missed sales and missed opportunities. Its so very important that you show enthusiasm and excitement when you are discussing your products or services, your goals, dreams or vision. You have to be passionate about what you got going on, if you expect someone else to believe in it and in you. If you are in business you must be a student for life. You should always be reading books, listening to audio cds and watching videos on sales, marketing, advertising and communication skills. Every single day, if you want to be great and looked upon as an expert and specialist in your particular field.

You must expect to win in every area of your life. Remember what ever you can imagine in your mind, you can create in your life, it's a beautiful thing to bring an idea to life. It's a beautiful thing to make something from nothing. It all starts with a thought. So do not doubt yourself or your abilities ever, instead continue to push yourself so that you will continue to improve and get better and better. So I close this chapter by saying continue to sell yourself on yourself every single day. And after you have built this daily consistent disciplined habit, then you must share this principle with everyone that you love and want the best for. Remember we are all called to love, encourage and support each other. I love you and let's continue to grow, let's continue to win because we are successful, we are winners.

5th Chapter

How to Apply All You Learned

You have learned so much through the years and it's a good possibility that you might only be using 1% of what you know on a consistent basis. We always use the phrase if you knew better than you would do better. But in most cases you do know better but you still don't do better. The question you must ask yourself is why? Why are you not doing better? Remember successful people ask themselves the tough questions. Successful people do not run from their problems. Instead successful people solve problems, successful people find solutions quickly. You are not stupid, but if you compare all that you know, all that you have learned throughout your life with the results you have been receiving, you might think that you are in fact stupid because you are not fully applying all that you know, to every area of your life. We about to transform right now simply because now we understand and see that we know so much but are achieving so little. You have received so much information throughout the years, that you do not realize how to filter what's important and what's not. From now on I challenge you to try out and apply every bit of new information that comes your way. Because the key to changing you and your situation is in your response to new information and advice that you receive. Remember 1 new idea, 1 new principle or concept can shift the course of your entire life. So recognize and be aware of what's coming your way. You must keep your ears, eyes and heart open at all times to be in a position to receive and then respond accordingly.

We all started out crawling, then walking and eventually before long we were running all over the place. We are always growing, we are always progressing. We must look at ourselves as our #1 investment. So we must constantly add value to ourselves, because if we are not consistently investing in ourselves then we will not continue to win. Winners invest in themselves all the time because winners recognize that in order to consistently win time after time after time then its going to take investing. You are your best asset. So if you are not constantly pouring into yourself then you are at a major disadvantage. Just take a moment to think about all the lessons you learned through the years. Think about all the hours and hours and hours of time you spent learning things. But compared to all the actions you have executed due to all the information you been receiving, you must admit that there is no comparison. You have been slacking and that's why you haven't been receiving the results you desire. You have to be sick and tired of barely getting by. You have to get sick and tired of steady wishing. You have to get sick and tired of always talking about what you going to do but never do. Truth be told, if you just did what you said you was going to do, then you will be further ahead and in a better position than you are in now. What I do is when I learn new stuff, I try it and put it into action to see if it's true, to see if it actually works. Its a rather simple process and you begin to learn what you can incorporate into what you got going on and what you need to dismiss because it doesn't apply to you. Some people, well truthfully most people will miss out on life changing information and advice because they don't realize that the valuable information can come from any one. It does not matter who the messenger is, but what matters is that you take a moment to open your heart, your eyes and your ears to receive the message, who ever it's coming from and then to test it for yourself. Then and only then will you know rather its valuable or not. But if you dismiss information before testing it because it sounds foreign to you, then at that moment you can be classified as a fool. Because in essence the majority of people will miss out on opportunities because they have a "I know that" mentality. Judging a person because of looks, financial status or education level can cause you to miss out on 1 idea that could possibly shift the course of your life. Example, it's possible to learn how to be a millionaire from a homeless person, sounds strange but idea's backed with actions can cause elevation and promotion rapidly. Sometimes you can learn more from a homeless person than you can from a multi-millionaire. So do not discredit any one that comes in your life. Instead develop the habit of listening and then testing all new information that you receive. I believe if you look down on people then you will be looked down on. But if you lift people up, then in return you will be lifted up. Make it a habit to respect everyone you come in contact with. Remember no one likes to feel rejected and everyone wants to be accepted and loved. That's why it's so very important to respect each others differences. And make sure you make people feel important, because everyone is important and we all need each other. It's so important that you understand and apply these principles so that it becomes a lifestyle and part of your daily living. Quick story, a few months ago I got 20 $25 gas gift cards, to pass out to bless people randomly on the streets. Funny thing is that majority of people told me no, not even knowing what they are saying no to. Not knowing they are getting ready to be blessed. Everyone is so busy now a days it seems like. It saddens me that so many people will say no, not even knowing what they are saying no too. People have been conditioned and programmed to say no, on a regular basis. Without even having all the information presented to them. I'm convinced that lots of people miss out on blessings and opportunities because they are to busy to take a moment to just listen. Remember we are all called to love, encourage and support one another. (I say this all day everyday, at least 100 times a day because I believe it to be true with everything that's in me.) One of the simplest yet most important things you can personally do to make a difference in the lives of others, is to simply listen and to encourage. Actually lets make another commitment or declaration to encourage one another at all times. Because you never knew what someone is going through. Remember people are hurting and you do not want to be the person that adds to the hurt. Instead you can be the person that eases the pain. You have to look for opportunities to help others and to be a blessing to others. We all need help from time to time, in one area or another. Remember it's better to be in a position to give, than it is to be in a position to have to receive. My hope is for you to try out the principles and values in this book and I believe that you will encounter life changing experiences. I believe that change will take place in every area of your life. And I believe you will do more, have more and be more. So I speak peace, favor, increase and promotion over your life. I speak creativity and purpose to manifest in your life. I believe you can stop any bad habits or vices you have, that you know are hindering your growth and messing up your relationships. I believe if you are sincerely and genuinely ready for change. I believe change is taking place for you right now and things are lining up for you. So get excited and please apply these principles daily to your life.

I want to thank you again for making an investment in yourself by buying this book. I'm sure it added value to you and that's what it is all about. Now lets go deeper.

Another principle I have to mention is we live in a cashless society where majority of people do not carry cash and only carry debit cards and credit cards. My suggestion to you is to always carry some cash even though it's not popular. Alot of people say they do not carry cash because if they get robbed then the robber would just be practicing because they don't have any cash on them. Well lets look at it from a different perspective, what if the robber get's so pissed and upset that you do not have any cash, that the robber then results to using badly harm on you or even killing you. You don't know what amount of pressure that robber is up against and 1 wrong thing can trigger something that would cause a terrible outcome. So it's better to have a little cash on you at all times, just for emergencies. I know this was an extreme example but the only reason I used it, is because I literally hear it all thee time, like everyday almost. People are so fearful for one reason or another. When I think about fear, I think about thinking about something negative that's going to happen that 9 times out of 10 is not even going to happen. We need to stop being so fearful. It's smart to be cautious, but being extra fearful is not good. As you become more confident with yourself, then the fears will start to disappear.

Quick story recently I was in the post office getting ready to ship out some items. It was a long line about 15-20 people in front of me. I was thinking dang I'm going to be in here for about 20 minutes. Then the cashier screamed is there anyone paying with cash. And low and behold I was the only one out of everyone in the line that had cash. So I was granted favor and was able to walk from the back of the line, to the front of the line. So the moral of the story is keep a little cash on you, so you will be positioned to seize certain opportunities that others will miss because they are not prepared. I believe it's so important to always have a little cash on you because even though majority of businesses accept credit cards. There still will be situations where you need some cash on you or you will miss out on a opportunity. So please take heed to this advice and start keeping a little cash on you. It's so important that we be on point at all times. You have to understand everything you learn in life is for a reason, the good and the bad. So be grateful and appreciative for everything you have been through so far, because it has prepared you for where you are now.

Another thing is you should always have at least 2 sources of income. So if you currently only have 1, then please work on another. You owe it to yourself to have a few sources of income. That will allow you to be more secure. So many people are getting laid off, so many people are loosing their businesses. It's so important to have at least 2 things you are working on simultaneously. If you are new to having an additional source of income, I suggest you choose something that you can easily incorporate into what you already got going on. That way you can flow smoothly while building both. It's important to have leverage because we only have so much time, so we must be very smart at what we decide to invest our time, energy and efforts into. Another thing is you have to pay your bills, you have to pay who you owe. You must have integrity about yourself. Because if you are constantly cheating people then shame on you. If you think you slick and you constantly conjure up ways to get over on people, then shame on you. If you owe someone, do not avoid them. Have integrity and set up some type of payment arrangement. You can not run from your problems, you must face them. So you must have a desire to do better. I'm glad I have great credit because it allows me to get what I want on terms. It's so important that you are always working on improving your credit. Remember your credit is your reputation, so if you owe everyone and you are not paying then know that that's not cool. You are wrong and you need to stop it and handle your responsibilities. Don't ever be satisfied with average credit, always work on making improvements. Don't ever be satisfied being broke or barely getting by, because money is available to you. If you apply the principles and values discussed in this book then your finances will improve. If you take heed to the mindset and attitude that's needed to ignite change in your life, then every area of your life will improve for the better. That's good news, I know you are open to change or you would not have even picked up this book. That's why I titled it what I did, for that specific reason. So I know this is your time, I know this is your season for increase, elevation and promotion. So all the new commitments and declarations you have made, must be kept because you are getting ready for your best life now. So embrace it and know you deserve it because you are so valuable and so worth anything you desire. Success is yours, so claim it and be willing to put the work in every single day because operating at 50% won't cut it. You must put forth 100% energy and effort to everything you say and do. So stay motivated, stay encouraged because a new change for you is worth it. You have the power to change your situation, you must simply neglect all the distractions in your life and just stay focused on doing the things that are necessary to get you the results you desire. If you are going to complain, do not complain to people. Complain to yourself and discuss with yourself the issues and then formulate a plan of actions that would lead to a solution. You will get better results if you write out your complaints that you have, on a sheet of paper and then write out different solutions then try different one's to see which one works best for you. Don't believe it works, just try it and see. It's something powerful happens when you write it out and when you see it. Suddenly your mind conjures up solutions, it's amazing how it works but it in fact works for real.

Another thing that is extremely important is that you listen and pay attention to yourself. Notice how you feel when certain things happen in your life. You must know what makes you smile. You must know what makes you cry. You must know what makes you laugh. And you must know what makes you sad. You have to listen to how your body responds to different things. You have to listen to how you react in different environments. You must be a bit sensitive to yourself, so you can be aware of yourself. Because you could be living with your self for all these years but not even truly know yourself. Spend time getting to know yourself more, because you have to live with you, for the rest of your life. So you need to be sold out on yourself. You need to love yourself 100% if you are going to be truly as powerful as you can be. If you get to the point where you can truly say you love yourself 100%, flaws and all, then you are positioned to having your best life now. And in all actuality even the way we look at perceived flaws is distorted because we can only think we have flaws when we are comparing ourselves to someone or something. But that's one of the tricks of society and our environment to try to get us to think we are suppose to be a certain way or look a certain way. We actually been programmed to think we have so many flaws, that's a trick to get you to buy more stuff that will supposedly fix the perceived flaws. If someone came to you and said you are perfect in every way. The first thing you would think is no I'm not because I got this problem and that problem. It's easy for us to see what we think is wrong with us. But in the midst of everything, the perceptions, and how we see ourselves in spite of all the images that bombard us all day everyday. We must know for ourselves, with out a shadow of a doubt that we are amazing, we are phenomenal, we look good, we feel good and we love ourselves inspite of it all. That's why it's important that we actually compliment ourselves as well.

As you are reading I want you to think about all the lessons you have learned in the past and how you can actually apply the lessons learned to what you currently got going on. Also as you are reading I want you to write down all the new principles and figure out how you can start applying them immediately so that you can start seeing the results. Because this information is life changing if you take action now. It's not by accident that you are reading this right now with all the pressure you are dealing with. I speak peace into your life right now. I speak increase and promotion into your life right now. And I speak a willingness to change your mindset and attitude right now, in what ever area's that might need improvements, so that you will be positioned to get better results.

Remember to get better you have to want to get better. There is a slim possibility that you will get better by chance. It usually doesn't happen that way. You get better by actually making a choice, by making a decision to want to get better. Then you must follow through, because success in every area of your life depends on your ability to follow through.

If you have a dream and you been steady putting it off because you are coming with excuse after excuse after excuse. Make a declaration to yourself right now and tell everyone around you that you have no more excuses and you are getting ready to pursue your goals and dreams. After you have made this new declaration, it's no turning back, you have to move forward and make it happen. Because it's show time for you for real. I believe in you.

I believe you got what it takes, I'm starting to get excited for you because I sense this time you are going to be empowered to make it really happen. Its showtime for you.

Now I'm about to share with you what I do every single time when I'm trying to sell a product or service. This advice I'm about to give you works. So make sure you use it and be real when you use it because this is so powerful. I'm giving you advice from my heart because I love you and I love everyone that I sell anything to. Because I do not sell anything that I don't believe 100% that it would add value to who I'm selling it to. I sell what I know will make a difference in the lives of people. Now get ready to receive all the advice I'm getting ready to share with you, that I use every single day and it works. First you must have the right mindset and attitude when you are getting ready to sell your products or services. When you have a potential customer or client in front of you the goal is to always make a win win connection. You can not prejudge anyone because you do not know who can buy your product or service. One of the worst things you can do is prejudge and assume someone can't buy what your selling. Shame on you if you have that mindset or attitude, you are an amateur that think you are a pro. Remember everyone can buy what you got to sell or they know someone that can. This is how you must see each and every person that you come in contact with. Remember any new customer can be the one that leads to millions in sells. So you must act as if each new customer is that one because you don't know who they are, or who they know. So you must treat everyone as vip because they are vip. Never have the mindset that you are to good for your customer because they will detect that and not buy any thing from you. People love to buy from people that make them feel important. So you have to, have to make your customers feel important, loved and appreciated. My goal is to always make a connection that will build a relationship in a few minutes that will seem like we been knowing each other for years. I do this very well and I'm going to teach you how to as well. But you must be loving, you must be nice and you must be genuine and likeable in order to make this connection. You must have the customers best interest at heart and you must be willing to not make the sell, if you realize through conversation that your product or service will actually not be a good fit for them. At that point you switch gears and ask for a referral. The customer will respect you so much that they will remember you for life because you had enough integrity to let them know in fact that your product or service would not be a perfect fit. (This will happen from time, to time and it's ok, it's part of business.) You must be a bit aggressive in the sales process. I have learned in most cases that it is in fact better to be a bit aggressive than it is to be passive. So have 100% confidence in yourself and in your products or services. You must be enthusiastic and passionate as you are explaining the benefits of your products or services. You must remember through the whole sales process you goal is to always add value to what you are saying, because once perceived value has exceeded actual value then you will make a sale usually everytime. Example if your product or service is $100 but you have displayed and communicated that your product or service is worth 5 to 10 times as much then obviously the customer will buy because they are getting a product or service worth $500-$1,000 that they are only paying $100 for. People buy because of an emotional connection, because of a feeling so you have to keep this in mind during the sales process. You can use tricks and gimmicks to sell people but it will not work. The tricks, the gimmicks the games will come back to bite you in the butt. Slick selling is not good selling, dishonest selling is not good selling. Good selling is having integrity about yourself and your products or services. If you feel that if your product or service will not make a difference in the life of the customer or client, then you should not be selling it. Yes I said it, if you do not love what you are selling you do not need to be selling it. If you are selling something that's hurting people instead of helping them, then shame on you. That means you are indeed part of the problem. You have to sell what's right not what's wrong. You have to promote something that helps, not something that hurts. You also must understand that selling is a great profession so when you become great at it, then you will never have to worry about making money. Because when you learn the skill of selling you will be able to make so much money, that there is no limit. So selling is extremely important because it gives you more options. Remember no one likes a pushy salesman, so it's a way to be aggressive and confident without being pushy. Another thing is you must look like you can afford what you are selling. Because even though you shouldn't judge your customers or clients. You must know that they are in fact judging you so make sure you look presentable. Nice hair done, smelling good, looking good, feeling good, dressed neat and clean shoes are important because customer are either directly looking or indirectly looking and paying attention to those things. So always try to look your very best please. Also remember people are not really impressed with big words, so even if it seems like they are, in most cases they are not. So try to keep your words simple and relatable and kind of mimic your customers vocabulary, that will bring out that like ability factor that will lead to a connection being made. It's important to let your customer feel that you appreciate their time and consideration of choosing you. A great salesman provides an enjoyable experience through the whole process understanding the customer is getting ready to invest with you and spend there hard earned money with you, while they had many many other options. You must appreciate the opportunity that they are giving you to earn their business. I want to take this moment to thank you again for your love and support. I so appreciate the fact that you made the investment to buy this book and I'm going to need your love and support on future books and projects as well ok. You see how I just showed you that I appreciate your love and support. You see how that made you feel good. That's an example of what you must do in the sells process. I hope your getting this because this is good stuff and if you implement this then you will see how valuable it is. My goal is for you to get better. My goal is for you to achieve more. My goal is for you to have increase in every area of your life. My desire is for you to be so very successful that it blows your mind. I love you so much and truly want the best for you and everyone that stands to benefit from you improving and making the necessary changes that you need to make to get more results in your life. Now lets go through an example of what I do when I'm getting ready to meet a stranger or potential customer or client. When I first meet a new person I start off with a compliment. Remember everyone loves to receive a compliment. I simply compliment on what I really feel is nice. Rather its sunglasses, earrings, hair cut, hair due, make up, jacket, clothes, car, shoes, purse what ever it is that stands out to me. It actually happens naturally because I do it everyday. So I don't know in advance what I'm going to compliment, I just know I'm going to give a compliment. So whatever it is I just give the compliment. Then I give a brief description of what I do. I'm always excited and passionate as I describe what I do. (Initial description should be no longer than 15-30 seconds.) Then you must ask the stranger or customer for there name. This is so important that you get there name. (Also throughout the whole conversation remember to address them by there name this is so powerful.) Then you give them your name. This is important to set it up this way because you compliment them first, that is going to make them feel good and it let's them know you recognized what they took time to make look nice. Then you passionately jump right into what you do and what your working on briefly. That lets them know you are actually excited about what your selling and what you got going on. It shows the customer that it is extremely important. Then you are keeping it brief to, then ask for there name, that's letting them know that you care about them and want to actually know there name instead of going on and on about what your trying to sell. Then you let them know your name so that they know who you are and who they are dealing with. Then you say "I have been feeling great today "How are you feeling? Most cases they will say great as well. Then you say wonderful, I'm definitely glad to hear that. If they say they are not feeling good or they start complaining about something. Take a brief moment to show some empathy. Acknowledge there feelings. (Don't baby them because no one wants to get babied, but everyone wants to get babied. LOL some of you will get that and some of you it will go over your head. It's ok, lets stay focused it's all love.) Depending on what your products or services are, will depend on how you set up the next part of the process. Because in some cases it's good to go right in and ask the customer questions first. But then in some cases it's good to go straight in to the benefits of your products or services to add that valuable so that the customer understands the quality of what you provide and how dealing with you is the best choice. No matter which way you do this process, both need to be done that's for sure. Make sure that you are looking your customer in there eyes, this is a sign of confidence, authority and power and people love it in most cases. As you are looking the customer in the eyes, you should try to connect with them in such a way that they feel your heart and you must speak to them in a way that touches them emotionally. You must connect with the heart, because people do not care about how much you know, until they know how much you care. Through the process you can not and I repeat you can not be the one doing all the talking. You must be a great listener to be effective in the sales process. So listen, listen, listen and listen some more. Another thing that I do and it works very well for me. I actually let the customer know in what way there support will benefit me as well. I also let the customer know what future things I'm working on as well. This will give the customer a sense of knowing that they are working with the right person. You have to hype yourself up a bit in the process because it gives you more credibility. And people love to buy from people who are credible. So always tell great stories and give testimony's from other customers or clients that love your products or services. This is so very important in the process. You must share great customer reviews that you have received in the past. You must show them pictures if possible or show something physically that will be visible so they can link that with what you are saying and it adds credibility. Also you must give them a testimony about yourself as well and let them know that you use and you love the products or services your selling. This is so very important as well, don't assume that they don't want to hear it from you because they will feel as if you are trying to sell them. Don't think about it that way, please don't. It's so important that you share your personal feelings about what your selling and if you have family and friends as well that support your products or services. Make sure you share that as well because from a customer stand point, that speaks volumes. So I'm giving you advice that works and that will take you to the next level and that will put more money in your bank account. So you must apply what I'm saying, all you have to do is try these principles and you will see for yourself how valuable they are. They will literally change your life, change your business and change your relationships for the better. So take heed because this is good stuff. Matter of fact lets make another commitment that you will apply these new principles and values to your life. Because if you are not willing to make the commitment, then you are not ready for the results that will come your way. I only say this because I love you and I want you to win in every area of your life. We are a team and together we going to win. Actually I'm going to do something different that no author will do. Send me a text right now, that says "We will win." (My number is (773) 563-5880) and we will win yall because we are winners.

I want you to understand that we are partners. Because you decided to support me with making the necessary investment to buying this book. So we have to continue to win because to me success is giving back. I will discuss that in the next chapter. But I'm giving you what I know that works, so I say again if you put into action the principles, values and secrets layed out in this book. Then your life will change and never be the same. As you are in the sales process never ever be afraid of going for the close. Never be afraid of asking for the business. Never be afraid of asking for the money. Sometimes you can go for the close quickly and sometimes it will take a little longer. Depending on what you sell. Depending on what your products or services is. Also make sure that after you sell your product or service make sure to always follow through and follow up.

It's important to make your new customer or client feel like part of the family. Remember no one wants to be rejected and everyone wants to be accepted. So you must accept peoples criticism. You must accept peoples questions and you must accept peoples difference of opinions. You can always let people know that you feel where they are coming from and that you have felt that way before as well but that you have found out that this way works best. (And then you give examples.) This is the feel, felt found close. I learned this in some sales training years ago and it works.

Also remember through the sales process to always keep track of how the new customer or client heard about you or your products or services. Because if it was a referral it will always be an easier process. Remember if it was in fact a referral you must bring that up as well because that will bring about extra credibility.

If you are soliciting people for your product or service and they are steady saying no. Without you even getting the chance to share some information with them. You must say this "Let me show you what you're saying no to, it will only take a minute and it just might be something you or someone you know is interested in. So please give me 1 minute of your time so at least you will know what you are saying no to." Saying this phrase has made me thousands and thousands of extra money that I would not have made, if I would have just accepted a no as a no and left it at that. You have to be a little aggressive or you will literally miss out on so many sells. Because people are busy, people don't have much time. People in general hate soliciting that's why you see posted on so many stores and homes no soliciting. A little secret some homes put the sign up because the man in the house, knows his wife or woman likes to shop and spend money. The sign is put up as a suggestion to past by this place because were not buying.

I personally still go to all stores that say no soliciting and all homes that say no soliciting. Because I look at what I do as promoting and not soliciting. And I have discovered that lots of places that have the no soliciting, actually end up buying from me. The key is to always smile because that is what gets you in the door. So many times people have told me, rather coming up to their car, home or place of business that the only reason that they opened the door is because I was smiling. So that's another principle, make sure that you smile, make sure you are friendly and make sure you are nice through the whole process. Do not be mean because its not productive. You can be firm though, because it is important to be firm and a bit bold during the process because that shows confidence. And people love to buy from confident people that's for sure.

Also if you work at a company that has a no soliciting sign and you hate soliciting. Recognize that the person you are turning away, could be a potential customer and could lead to more customers, more referrals and ultimately more money for you and for your company. So keep that in mind as well. Because if we are in business we all need more customers and more support. So treat everyone fairly and with respect if you are in business. I know for a fact that I could help more people that have shut me down on the streets. Some people have the mindset and mentality that they would not buy anything from anyone off the streets. And that's a sad mentality to have because you could be possibly shutting down something that could make a difference in your life. You could be possibly saying no to something, that could be the solution to all your problems and issues. You could literally be missing out on the best opportunity of your life because you are saying no and don't even know what you are saying no to. It's funny because I have a motivational cd I have and it's so powerful, life changing actually. And of course I understand everyone is not going to buy and it's a numbers game. I understand all these things, heck I been selling since I was a little boy. But I encounter some people that say "You can't motivate me your on the streets selling." I encounter this often and it's funny because society looks at the person on the streets selling body oils, cds, purses, face towels, candy etc. As less than them, they look down on the profession of selling in this format. Not understanding that it can be very lucrative option as well. I have so many stories, it's amazing some of the things I see and hear from people. You wouldn't believe some of the things I hear that people say. That brings me to my next point, try to always think before you speak it will take you far in life and you will end up with less regrets.

The other day a guy at a gas station told me that he couldn't learn anything from me. The guy said look at what I'm driving (it was some old school car probably worth about $6,000) The guy said he had his own place that he is renting. And that he makes $40,000 a year. (This guy looked to be in his 50's or maybe late 40's, and I'm 32 years old and maybe I look like I'm 18 years old. LOL But I'm married with 4 kids, just look young.) He judged me because he seen me on the streets and I was selling my motivational cd's and he assumed that I couldn't teach him anything because he assumed he made more money than me. (Fellas you have to check your ego, just because you are doing ok doesn't mean you can be rude to people. Ladies likewise you have to be nice and not have a stank attitude. Because we all can learn from someone. We all can grow and we all can do and be better.) I'm just really humble at all times but on this occasion, I had to let dude know who he was talking too. I tried to hold back but I had to let him know because he was so disrespectful. I had to let him know I drive a Cadillac Escallade which was parked a few feet away. I drive what most men dream about owning. I let him know I actually own 2 houses and there both paid for because I worked my but off to pay for them both. 1 property is a rental where I get rental income and other is property that me and my family live in. Majority of people my age do not have a home that they own let alone to have it free and clear. And dude was so proud of his $40,000 a year job. And I had to let him know that I made way more than him. So long story short I got my point across to that brother. So hopefully he won't be disrespectful to other people he see on the streets in the future. Now mind you, usually my character would not even allow me to go off like that. But on this occasion I did and it felt great. But I love what I do everyday, even the challenges that comes along with it. It's never a boring day in my life. Because I'm always working on my business and making things happen. And when I'm not working I'm always busy giving back and helping different communities. And rest of my time is spent with my wife and kids and enjoying family and life. I'm so grateful and appreciate for life and I hope you are as well. Remember you should never be bored because there is always something for you to be working on. Especially if you are an entrepreneur and in business. Also if you got kids I know they keep you plenty busy. Make sure as you take care your kids, and teach them and train them. Make sure you are paying attention to them as well, because we can learn so much from our kids. Look at how creative they are, look at how they do not take no for an answer. Look at how they constantly ask questions. And look at how they are excited to learn new things and how they are excited to try new things. So its a message in that, so always keep your eyes, ears and heart open to receive the messages that are right in front of you. Be encouraged, be motivated and it's a few more pointers I want to discuss in this chapter and then we going to move on to Giving Back and Legacy.

Do not allow the past mistakes you have made in the past to stop you from making new mistakes. And always feed on the things you have learned in the past. You have deposited in you many lessons learned. So now is the time to apply what you learned in the past and time to apply what you are currently learning as well. Life itself is a learning process, we all know this to be true. How you bounce back is what will make all the difference in your life.

So you must take initiative in life no matter who you are or what you do. If you got a job or a business you better be grateful because it's so many people that our out of work and have no income. So slow down on any and all complaining because I'm sure there are millions of people that would love to trade places with you. So be grateful and be appreciate but don't be satisfied because you still want to grow. So get motivated and get excited and get to work. Remember as I say all day everyday, we are all called to love, encourage and support one another. Look for ways that you can help others. Because if you have the ability or know how to help assist someone else and you decide not to because you are selfish. Then shame on you. Because you know better, you know what it feels like to be down and out. Everyone has experienced it temporarily, at one point or another. So be compassionate if you see someone else going through what you have been through in the past. But was able to over come through it all. Be loving and do not add more hurt to those that are hurting. Be kind and be generous when ever you have the opportunity to. Everyday I personally seek to make a difference with everyone that I come in contact with. I provide excellent customer service. I understand the importance of serving and realize the more people you serve the greater impact you have. With me it's deeper than money, I genuinely love people. I genuinely love to help people. I genuinely want us to win and I genuinely want to make a difference in the lives of others. I'm glad that I have found my purpose and my passion. I'm glad that I work on it every single day. I'm in a great place right now and my desire is for you to be in a great place right now as well. Because you deserve the best especially when better is available. At the same token I love to be served as well. I love to receive great customer service and I tip well. It's so important that you serve your customers well because if your in business or anything dealing with customer service and you got a stank attitude and you are wondering why things are not working out for you. Let me give you a hint, your attitude needs some adjusting and you know it. So if you know, that what you are currently doing is not working, then you really need to be open for change. It starts with changing of your attitude and mindset that we discussed a few chapters back. Another thing is you can not continue to blame others for your problems or issues. You must have personal accountability and you must be responsible for your life and the decisions you have made and your going to make. We all know that every decision we make will come with consequences rather good or bad. It's important that you think about this fact before you make each decision. You know you were born to win, the fact that you are alive right now when others are dying daily is proof that you got work to do. So you got to get to it, the slogan to live by is no stress, no drama and no confusion. It's also important that you treat yourself. Because if you are constantly doing everything for everyone else all the time and you haven't did anything for yourself lately. Then take some time real soon to just treat yourself, to whatever you want to. You deserve to treat yourself from time to time, it's ok it's so necessary. Especially when you are working hard everyday. If you are lazy on the other hand, then you do not deserve to treat yourself. Because being lazy will separate you from your goals and dreams. Laziness will rob you of the joys that come from working hard to achieve things. Being lazy is one of the most unproductive habits to have. People talk about workaholics, why I don't know because workaholics in most cases love there work, they just don't have balance. And balance is important to have overall success, in every area of your life. It's extremely important to have a strong work ethic and it's equally important to have some what of a balance, to incorporate family and play time into the success equation. You have to make sure that your family understands the sacrifices that must be made, while you are in the building process. You must let them know that you appreciate there support as you are putting in so much time in building your brand or building whatever it is that you are building that would benefit them. Also you have to make sure you include your family in the process, so they do not feel like you are leaving them out. (Rather they support you or not, still try to make attempts to include them during the process.) Remember anyone that supports what you are doing consistently deserves thank you gifts from time to time. Make it a habit of rewarding the people that love you and support your dreams and goals. Because that will always help things move along smoothly through the process. My suggestion is to be a great gift giver, it will give you favor and your people will appreciate it. Also remember you should always let everyone know who you are and what you do. And also if you got products make sure you keep them on you at all times or at least some information about your products or services, this is important. To me it's common sense, but I'm learning that to most people it's actually not. Majority of people just have products or services for sale during certain hours, which are what they consider work hours. Well if you are an entrepreneur and you are serious about growth, then you need to keep your products and/or info on you at all times. Yes literally 24/7 is ok, don't let anyone tell you it's weird to sleep with business cards in your pajamas. (Don't be laughing at me either. It's all love. And yes I do sleep with business cards. Also I do always have my products and information with me. It's just a habit because I sell all day everyday for real.) Another thing I must explain to you, is that you must be willing to be embarrassed if you want to be truly successful.

So yes it's going to take you getting out of your comfort zone all the time. Good news is eventually you will become comfortable being uncomfortable. You will have to be great at talking to strangers and new people all the time. Do not worry about being thirsty, it shows determination and the right people will respect it and support just because you made the attempt. When in doubt always try, because at the most awkward times and places is when people will actually support, so try to seize every opportunity that comes your way. Never be afraid to discuss your products or services. It does not matter what race. It does not matter what gender. It does not matter what financial status. It does not matter what education level. If you know that your products or services would be beneficial to them, then you must share. Everyone will not say no. You have everything to gain and nothing to loose, is how I see it. That's why I be thirsty to sell my items to anyone. Because I truly believe it's worth it. And I have witnessed the difference it makes in the lives of others. I have gotten back testimony, after testimony, after testimony with great results as to how powerful and life changing my products and services have been. I know I add value to peoples lives, so I'm never afraid to show my items. Because in my mind, you really need what I have to offer. In my mind you are crazy if you not buying from me. (LOL just playing, naw no I'm not. I crack myself up.) But all jokes aside you have to know your worth and know your value.

Time for another commitment please make this commitment if you are serious about change and improving in every area of your life. Just make the commitment to let everyone you come in contact with know who you are, what you sell and what you have going on and what you are working on. I repeat again you never know what difference one person can make in your life. So try to not let no one pass you by, without sharing what you need to share with them. I believe if you actually do this it will make the world of difference in your life and in your financial situation. So just try it and see what happens, I can assure you that you will meet way more amazing people, some that will support and some that will not support. So be willing to always put forth 100% energy and effort into making it happen. Because you got so many people that are depending on you. Now is the time for change. Now is the time to do what you got to do, regardless of how you feel. You got to get pass feelings and be on principles and values. Because you might not feel like putting that 100% efforts in each and everyday. But when you understand that you are now living by principles, and you got standards that govern your life then that will push you into your next levels of greatness.

You do not need people to validate you because now you are sold out on yourself, because you sell yourself everyday. Your validation comes from your confidence in yourself and in your ability to consistently make things happen. It's so important to be focused because then you are not pulled in so many different directions. Instead you are focused on the daily activities that must be implemented to reach your weekly goals. Successful people analyze how time is being spent. From now on there is no time to waste. You must be working while your working, so say goodbye to any slacking you used to do. Because now you are so focused, that you have no time for foolishness. No time for stress, no time for drama and no time for confusion.

I have learned that everyday is a great day. There are no bad days. (There are bad moment's but you have the power to shift a bad moment, by just deciding to remain positive in the midst of whatever is going on.) Do not allow a temporary setback or mistake to make you loose focus. Unsuccessful people always play the victim role. Unsuccessful people allow a temporary failure or lost to get them to loose hope. Unsuccessful people want people to feel sorry for them. Unsuccessful people get knocked down and take so long to get back up. If you think you are unsuccessful then this is what you do, because these are some of the characteristics. But if you know you are successful or you have a burning desire to be successful in every area of your life. Then you must make a commitment to not do what the unsuccessful people do because that's not you.

You can not worry about all the things you used to worry about. Because now you are focused, so when ever something pops up in your head that trys to get you off track or trys to get you to start worrying. Do this and it's going to sound strange and seems weird but it works. Talk to the problem or issue inside your head and say no thank you. Yes you are talking to the issues that pop up within and you are telling them no thank you. You must guard your mind and guard your heart when you are focused on being successful in every area of your life. This is also what you must do to resist lustful temptations. You tell yourself no thank you. It works for me and it will work for you also, if you start putting it into use. When you start doing this on a regular basis, you will soon notice you have way more discipline than you previously had in the past. So please get in the habit of trying it because it works.

The question you should ask yourself everyday is. How can I show more love to everyone in my life and how can I show more love to every new person that I come in contact with? We need to be love magnets. We all know we want to be loved, so let's be more loving. And I'm talking about genuine love not fake love. If you are going to be fake with your love, then you can keep that. Because with everything that's going on, you have to show real love because real genuine pure love is needed. Everyone is yearning to receive real love. So if you can be a loving person, that will give you a major advantage. So if you want an advantage, then make up in your mind and heart that you are going to love people, encourage people and support people every single day it must become part of you.

So from now on you have to apply all that you learn, so then you will know what works for you and what doesn't work. Don't assume that something doesn't work just because it sounds strange to you. Just test it out and see but you can't test it out with the mentality. Oh I know this doesn't work, I'm just going to do it to prove to myself that it doesn't work, to confirm I was right about this strange idea not working. That mindset is not acceptable. When you are applying new information that you learned you must put forth 100% energy, 100% effort and you must have the mindset even though this sound's strange I'm going to try it with 100% open mindness because this could be the very thing that could change my life forever. Remember new information, new strangers that come into your life, new attitudes and new mindsets is what can bring about total change and a total transformation to your life. So always be open to receive and always be open to executing that new information that you receive.

6th Chapter

Give back/Legacy

How do you want to be remembered? What legacy do you want to leave, way pass when you are dead and gone? What ways can you be giving back more? These and more are some of the questions that you must start asking yourself and you must start answering them as well. The reason why I say it like that is because some times we ask ourselves questions but we do not in fact answer them. Sounds strange but if you think about it, you will realize that you do it all the time.

If you are serious about being successful in every area of your life then your give back initiatives are going to have to be priority on your list. Also how you are going to be remembered is going to have to be priority on your list. These things are important to winners. These things are important to successful people. Loosers don't care about these things. Selfish people don't care about these things. But if you are a person that is built for success and built for change, then these things you will have to incorporate into the decisions you make on a daily basis because they go together hand and hand. It has to be important to you and keeping it on your mind, will actually allow you to make better decisions. It will allow you to be more disciplined and more focused as well.

I live to give back, to me life is about giving back. Life is about leaving a legacy for my family, the world and future generations that will come behind me. See when you have this type of mindset, then you do not have time for foolishness. Because you are committing to making a difference, lots of things you can not do. You have no time to be caught up in any scandals or rumors that are going on around you. Your name and your reputation is extremely important so you must make sure you are not doing anything that will make you out to be a fool. Because remember in time things will come to the light. And yes I know what you are thinking, we all make mistakes. Yes that's true but you need to be trying to avoid any and all mistakes that would put your name and your reputation in the dirt. Because once scandal and rumors hit you. It can take years and years to bounce back from that. So just make sure you are not doing anything foolish that will hurt you and your credibility. Actually make a declaration right now, if you are currently doing something that you know is not right. If you are currently doing something right now that if you get exposed, if you get caught up it will bring shame to you and your family. Then make a decision right now to stop. Now is the time for change. Now is the time to live right and be right. Now is the time to love yourself enough, to make any and all changes in your life so that you are representing yourself with the utmost love and respect. Please do what's right and put any and all foolishness behind you. Today is a new day if you are doing something wrong and you know its wrong. If you feel so bad about doing it now as your reading. Then just make the decision right now to stop. Because your life depends on it. If you truly want to be successful in every area of your life, do what's right be true to yourself starting now. I love you and only want the best for you. I want you to be loyal and I want you to be faithful to yourself. I want you to live by principles, values and standards. I want you to be happy, I want you to be loved and loving.

I want you to be secure within yourself that you want to be right. I want you to realize that you owe it to yourself, to be your best self. Do not allow feelings to control you because you know your feelings have gotten you in trouble plenty times before in the past. So today is a new day, today is a new you. When you picked up this book, you see it said "Stop Don't Buy This Book....... Unless You Are Ready For Change." You decided to buy this because you knew in the inside that you wanted to change. So let this be your opportunity to make all the changes that you need to make, to get things right and in order for yourself. You have read all the principles in this book, now is the time to apply. I'm excited for you, I love you. I appreciate you so much and I'm going to need your continued love and support on future projects as well so let's continue to win and learn together. OK.

Let's go through a few more things as far as give back and legacy is concerned. Then we got some pages of notes for you to write down all the notes and all the principles that are of value to you, that you are going to apply immediately. Then I'm going to discuss with you a few more things that I'm working on and then that will be the close. But I have enjoyed the time that we have spent together through these pages. I hope you can feel my heart and my desire for wanting you to win. I hope you get a sense of who I am because everything that I'm writing comes from me and from my heart. I'm open I'm successful and I'm happy and my desire is for you to be in a great place.

One of the things I do to give back, is I go to feed and clothe the homeless twice per month and I truly enjoy it. My desire is always for the people, because people are hurting. One act of kindness, one display of love, one encouraging word or even one sincere genuine smile can make the world of difference in someone's life.

On a different note make sure you have life insurance also, because it saddens me to see how many people do not have life insurance. It's important so if you do have it, then that's good business. But if you don't have it then just get it. That's all I'm going to say about that.

I have given back so much in the past and I will continue to give back. Giving back has become a part of me. I live to give, I literally wake up with the mindset and attitude to help everyone, I come in contact with. And I believe because of my consistent giving back, I'm granted favor so I will continue to do it because it works. I'm always depositing principles and values into my kids, so I know for a fact that they will be properly prepared for life and to be successful adults. I pour into my kids everyday because as a parent, we have a responsibility to train and set our kids up for success. You also must save some money, don't spend every dime you get its not productive. So take some time and come up with a strategic budget and game plan for your money. Get addicted to making deposits. And get hesitant to making withdraws. Be quick to save and slow to spend. Make sure you are consistently investing in yourself and in what you are working on. The key is to spend money wisely and not foolishly. As you make more and your in a position to get more of your wants then by all means do so. But while your in the building process remain disciplined with your money and with your time. Remember all the decisions you make now will lead to either your success or your demise. You want to stay making winning decisions because if you are to be determined to give back, then you can't be loosing all the time.

I talk to alot of people that use to give back all the time but they stopped because they seen some one miss use there generosity. Example they could have giving someone $5 on the streets for food and then come to find out, that person used the money for drugs or for alcohol. So they used that one incident as a reason to not give back to anyone ever. Do not allow one incident to stop you from giving back. Quick story about 2 years ago I pulled up to a stop light and I noticed the homeless person on the street begging for change. I looked down at his feet and he had no shoes on. Feet was looking rough. So I asked the guy what shoe size he wore, he replied size 11. So that was my size, I quickly took my shoes off of my feet and handed it out the window to give to him. Now what he said next blew my mind. He said I don't need those, that will mess me up. Wow, the light then turned green and I pulled off. But I still did not allow that bad situation to get me to stop giving. It still trips me out that it happened when I think about it. But by me giving back so much, I meet people that are rude and disrespectful even when I'm helping them. It happens but do not let that discourage you, because there are way more people that appreciate your efforts and your love. So continue to give back. Continue to help and be a blessing to others. Another thing is do not give up on the youth. It troubles me when I talk to some senior citizens and they are so disgusted with the youth that they have given up on the future generations. We have to not condemn our youth, but instead we must love, encourage, guide and support our youth. I'm begging you do not give up on the youth. Do not give up on a family member or friend that is hurting and going through a rough season in their life. Do not give up on yourself. Do not give up on your dreams. Do not give up on the possibilities. Instead remain positive, remain hopeful and remain determined to be successful in every area of your life.

You have made plenty of new commitments through out this book. Now were coming to a close. So now it's on you. So what are you going to do? You fully understand that you have options. You fully understand the mindset and attitude that will lead to change. You have heard my story and hopefully you have learned some things from that as well. You fully understand that you must sell yourself on yourself everyday. You fully understand that you must apply all you have learned. You fully understand the importance of giving back and legacy. Now in the next chapter you must write out notes and you must formulate your new game plan. Congratulations, I love you now take care of your business. You will be successful in every area of your life.

Notes/Goals:

Notes/Goals:

Notes/Goals:

Notes/Goals:

Notes/Goals:

Notes/Goals:

Notes/Goals:

Notes/Goals:

Notes/Goals:

Notes/Goals:

Authors Info/Ministry Info

William D. Madison Jr is the founder of Turn Up Your Praise Ministry. It's an outreach ministry. Where we go out everyday in different communities to encourage, inspire and show love to everyone we come in contact with. Next we plan on starting a program to help aspiring entrepreneurs to start their own business. We are currently having a fundraiser so your love and support is needed. So we can continue to make a difference in the lives of people. So we can continue to make positive impacts and changes into every community that we go into. So please make a contribution into this ministry, where we are actually on the streets everyday making a difference. You can make a donation on the website, which is. www.turnupyourpraiseministry. com or you can make checks or money orders payable to Turn Up Your Praise Ministry and mail them to our mailing address:

Turn Up Your Praise Ministry

P.O. Box 288343

Chicago IL. 60628

Thank you in advance for your love and support. I appreciate you and I believe as you sow a seed into this ministry. That others will support you and sow a seed into your vision, your dreams and your goals. God Bless You.

Turn Up Your Praise Ministry

P.O. Box 288343

Chicago IL. 60628

www.turnupyourpraiseministry.com

(773) 563-5880

turnupyourpraiseministry@gmail.com

william@turnupyourpraiseministry.com.

Thank You

Printed in the United States
By Bookmasters